Praise for ESP

"**ESP** is straight talk about a touchy subject: how to put your head and your heart together on the job. It's the art of doing business in a common sense way."

The Honorable Ann Richards
Former Governor of Texas

"At last someone has taken the mystery out of selling! Walter and Steve are the only people I know who can stand at the cutting edge—and see around the corner!"

William H. Gove, Founder & First President
National Speakers Association

"A super-terrific action manual, with practical ideas you can put to use immediately that'll make your life happier, healthier, and wealthier. A 'must' for every winner's library!"

Ed Foreman, Author, Speaker, Business Entrepreneur
Former U.S. Congressman (Texas & New Mexico)

"For anyone who has not had the pleasure of attending their Boot Kamps, let me tell you what the rest of us already know: the Hailey/Anderson duo are dynamic motivators. Now with this book, they go one better—articulating those powerful ideas and getting the reader completely and contagiously involved."

Erla Kay, Senior Publisher, Dental Group
Southam Communications, Inc.

D0967856

More Praise for ESP

"If you can only put one more thing in your briefcase, make sure it's a copy of **ESP**. This is the owner's manual everybody meant to tell you about but never did. Don't fly without it."

> **Scott Walker, Director of Sales, National Accounts**
> **Hyatt Hotels and Resorts**

"**ESP** exceeds the speed limit! In his first book, *Breaking the NO Barrier,* Texas marketing entrepreneur Walter Hailey broke all the rules with his powerful NEER selling strategies. In *The Everybody Search Plan,* the Hailey/Anderson team maps out the new Route 66 for business."

> **Red McCombs, CEO**
> **McCombs Automotive Group**

"This book offers a remarkable view on the way we work and the way we relate to the people with whom we work... it's a winner!"

> **Tom Friedberg, Chairman, President & CEO**
> **ACCEL International**

"Brilliant, wise and defiant, **ESP** will have you laughing your way into a new level of indispensability with your customers as well as your company. These master mavericks of marketing are just what we need in these down-sized times."

> **Tommy Murray, President & CEO**
> **Murray Enterprises, Inc., dba Mailboxes, Etc.**

The Everybody Search Plan

The Everybody Search Plan

40 Common Sense and Easy-to-Implement Ideas to Get Everyone in Your Company Focused on Creating More Happy Paying Customers, Clients, Patients, Buyers or Whatever You Call the People Who Do Business with You

by Steve Anderson & Walter Hailey

THE EVERYBODY SEARCH PLAN
40 common sense and easy-to-implement ideas to get
everyone in your company focused on creating more happy
paying customers, clients, patients, buyers or whatever you
call the people who do business with you.

Published by Planned Marketing Associates, Inc.,
Hunt, Texas

For Ordering Information Call 1-800-HUNT-TEX

ISBN: 1-882-306-11-2

Library of Congress Catalog Card Number: 96-069-131

Printed in the United States of America

Contents

Dedication   v
Preface   vii
Introduction: A Word to Managers   xi

1 Broadcast Your CBS   1
2 The Parrot Principle   5
3 Be Your Own Most Committed Customer   8
4 The Love Connection   11
5 Know Your ICP   15
6 Position Power With Your Prospects   17
7 Reaching Out for Repeaters   20
8 Extend Your Repeater Reach   23
9 Add an E   25
10 The Law of Seven Circles   29
11 The Sphere of 250   32
12 Opening Up the "Help Line"   34
13 Speak Out   37
14 Be a Spark Plug   40
15 Filling the Obligation Vacuums   42
16 "Leave the Gate Open"   45
17 Give Yourself Away   47
18 "Collecting All Cards"   50
19 Two By Two Leverage   52
20 The Never Ending Search   54
21 Find a Partne(e)r   56
22 Bear Good News   58
23 "PEP" Squad (Promote Every Partner)   60

24 Spread the Good News About
Your Customers 63
25 Become a Creative (Re)Source
for Good Ideas 65
26 A Gatherer & a Sower Be 67
27 Fill Your Shoes & Find Some New Ones 69
28 Be a Private I 71
29 "All I Know Is What I Read in the Papers" 73
30 Help Me Count the Ways We Can Help 75
31 I Hear You, But How Do You Really Feel? 77
32 The Million Dollar Phone Call 79
33 Think BESA 82
34 Be a Pain Reliever, Not Just
a Problem Solver 84
35 Spread Cheer, Not FEAR 86
36 Inside Master Mind 88
37 Be a Transitional Thinker 90
38 Outside Master Mind 93
39 Mentoring 95
40 Keep Your Antennae Up 97

Glossary of Acronyms 99

this book is lovingly dedicated
to every person who has ever
worked on faith without evidence
and in turn created his or her own bright future

Preface

Every organization in America today has been flattened. Much of middle management is history. The work ethic, which used to be the rule of the day, no longer separates the great from the good because the only people left in most organizations are those who have a work ethic—if they don't have one, they're already gone!

The common denominator among these survivors of outsourcing, downsizing, and computerization is this: they get results. And the one result they have in common is in *attracting, creating and retaining happy paying customers, clients or patients who:*

a) pay more than it costs to get them;

b) repeat purchasing your company's products/services;

c) refer others.

These are the overall objectives of every organization.

Whether you drive the truck or the company itself, whether you've been with the firm all your life or are just starting out, whether your function is administrative or front line service, you had better **become committed to creating more qualified, less resistant buyers.**

That is why we at Planned Marketing Associates have been asked to write this handbook—to help you, no matter what you do within your organization, to develop the skills so that you continuously add value and contribute to the growth and profitability of the company.

For some people the ideas we share will confirm, challenge and expand what they are already doing; for others, these notions will amount to nothing short of a revolution in thinking, a revolution in outlook to match the revolution in business.

You must become a source and a resource to others!

Advancements in computers and telecommunication are challenging every assumption about who and how and where and when we go to work. Global markets and new technologies are doing away with the old paradigms for job security and career success. It's no longer possible to live a compartmentalized life. Work is not something you go to for eight hours a day but a state of mind you exercise all the time everywhere you go. Because the face of business is changing more drastically than it ever has before—and more rapidly—*have the attitude that you are in business for yourself.*

"Unlike the organization man, who pursued his career safely ensconced in a corporation's inner workings," writes Nobel laureate Arno Penzias, "tomorrow's workers must seek action." This handbook is that plan of action.

We call it **E**verybody **S**earch **P**lan for many reasons. First of all, it involves *everyone* in the company, without exception, not just management or the sales and marketing team. Secondly, it's a *search*; the mission is to seek out ways to bring new customers and new ideas continuously to the company. Thirdly, it's a *plan*, not just an attitude adjustment; it's a tried and true system that produces practical results. It has not only made us millions of dollars, but it is the *secret to our enjoyment in working together as a team* as well.

That's where the Extra Sensory Perception comes from—when the minds and hearts of everyone on board the company are focused on the same goal, the effect is exponential. The whole becomes much greater than the sum of its parts.

With these forty easy-to-implement ideas, you will plug into your company's mission and add value, allowing you to:

- *get more praise and recognition for what you do;*
- *create a higher pay potential;*
- *respond more effectively to challenge;*
- *increase job satisfaction; and*
- *insure financial and emotional security.*

Don't just meet the challenge. **Arm yourself with the information and skills you need to come out on top.**

Introduction

A Word to Managers

If you're not in management, turn directly to Idea #1.

If you are in management, read this introduction of twelve tips first. It's about attitude.

A chain is only as strong as its weakest link. In order to develop an ESP environment it takes the commitment, dedication and focus of the entire company, *including the team leader*. Here's what managers can do to insure—and inspire—an ESP spirit in your work place.

1

Eliminate the difference between selling and doing.

Everything everyone does sells the company. Most owners—and most managers—fail to teach ALL their team members that *the only purpose* of a business is to create *happy paying customers who repeat and refer and pay more than it costs to provide them the service.*

Everyone on board, everyone drawing a paycheck, shares this same goal. Non-sales personnel have been isolated for too long. They must be brought into the sales and marketing loop. A worker who has either direct or indirect contact with customers and prospects must be schooled in positioning and selling the company. Not only will they help add value, but if they remain unguided they can—and will—destroy sales and profits.

The real ESP is not Everybody Search Plan.

The real ESP is Everybody *SELL* Plan.

2

Get everyone in the company on the same page.

This *invisible sales force* needs to join forces with the sales and marketing team, and not allow apparent differences to divide them. The biggest problem for many companies is the antagonism which flares up between departments. The production team, the shipping and receiving team, the accounting team should not be at odds with the sales team.

Be a leader in helping everyone focus on the common purpose . . . harmoniously. All must work together.

3

Why do people work?

The first motivation is for *recognition*. The second is for *challenge*. The third is for *personal growth*. The fourth is for *money*. If the first three are not present, the only motivation an employee has is that paycheck. To increase motivation start at the top:

4

Develop a system of meaningful recognition.
Make an ESP award system. *People will repeat behaviors that are rewarded.* Team members must get recognized in front of their peers.

Whatever is most appropriate—a plaque or certificate suitable for framing given at a company awards dinner by a senior officer; an extra paid holiday; an Employee of the Month program announced through the company newsletter; a Weekly Brag Sheet posted on the bulletin board; a special parking place for the month—*the program must be prestigious and worthwhile* enough to touch that highest motivation in us all, the need to be praised.

5

Don't take the credit, give the credit.
Gain the reputation as a collaborator, not a dictator. Instead of coming up with the best solution yourself, ask for input. *Let others show you what they can do.*

Bum Phillips, former head coach of the Houston Oilers, shared the following story at one of our Boot Kamps.

"Bear Bryant, the famous football coach, used to think through every play the team used that failed. He'd work out all the angles on the blackboard, then erase it and invite the entire team to sit down and figure out how to fix the play. Like Socrates, he'd guide with questions until finally one of the players would speak the correct answer. Not only did the player, not the coach, become the hero and enjoy the recognition, but every player present was thinking."

Bear Bryant didn't need the praise. He needed thinking athletes on the football field. And that's what he got. And that's why he's praised as one of the greatest coaches in the history of the game.

6

ESP is not only about sales; it's about performance.

Once everyone on board is thinking how to increase sales, how to position the company, how to create add-ons for customers, how to niche market, don't stop there. Encourage the formation of Master Mind groups and think tanks.

Get people to meet for brainstorming sessions.

What should they be thinking about? Ways to increase their effectiveness in what they do for the company.

- Who came up with the profitable (sales without selling cost) idea that flyers, with order forms attached, be included with all shipments to customers? A shipping clerk.

- The idea for placing "take one" dispensers in strategic locations throughout the store? A secretary.

- A customer-calling plan offering information about services selected customers were not aware of and not using? A bank teller.

- Using the toll free 800 number? A mail room clerk.

7

If you've created performance standards, replace them with a model of constant improvement.

When team members work to reach certain standards for acceptable performance, their mind set is automatically limited. They are thinking the wrong way. Once they reach the quota of what's expected of them, once they've found a way to make no mistakes, they've ceased being creative.

In order to have on-line team members helping evolve the company, they've got to change their mind set.

They must broaden the scope of their thinking. Instead of performance expectations, they need to be concerned with, "How can I help make this product or service bigger, better, faster and more satisfying to the customer?"

8

What is the cost of an idea?

Absolutely zero. It doesn't cost the company a penny. Nevertheless, getting people to think is the greatest asset you've got as a manager. Though it never shows on your balance sheet, *the greatest resource you have is thinking people on the front line.* Inspire their confidence. The folks in the trenches know what works and what doesn't. They know what and where 90% of the real trouble is and how to fix it. Your job is getting them to tell you.

9

Make it easy to submit ideas.
People need to know their suggestions matter.

Once encouraged to think, *team members need to know that their suggestions will be collected, reviewed and responded to in an orderly and timely fashion.*

It is crucial that "the suggestion box" be strategically placed so that people get in the habit of using it.

10

Solve the problem at the lowest level possible.
Make it company policy that *you can't point out a problem without offering at least two or three solutions, one of which is inexpensive.*

Increased perception leads to increased responsibility. Help people create closure on a task by getting them to think not only in terms of what's wrong but what are the best ways to make it right. Guide them in the development of their judgment by making them accountable for helping solve the problems they uncover.

11

Help your team lead itself to glory.

Meet with your team every week at a regular time. What will they discuss? *This handbook!*

Each week make sure one of the team members in your department presents one of the 40 ESP ideas to the rest of your team. Let that front line person do the talking. Let him or her explain the idea and lead the discussion to follow.

The one who teaches is the one who learns the most.

Remember KIS/MIF: *Keep it simple; make it fun.*

12

Make sure your ESP effort succeeds.

How do you do that? *Make one person within your department accountable* for the ESP environment. Everyone needs to be responsible for making contributions to the effort, but the program will rise or fall based on the individual who is accountable for the total result.

Broadcast your CBS

People don't buy features; they buy benefits, they buy what you can do for them. If you're not totally plugged in to what your company, what your product and service can do for people, then it will be very difficult for you ever to convince anybody that you're doing any good.

Sit in the chair of your customer for a minute. What does your company do that no one else does for that person? What makes what you offer extraordinary?

We call this **CBS: Compelling Benefit Statement.**

Here's what Betty Waller, our chief company accountant, answers when asked what she does for a living: "I generate financial statements for a marketing company that guarantees a 20% increase in our customers' businesses or they pay us nothing. If their bottom line isn't better by a fifth, they never even end up in my financial statement!"

Because her **focus** is **on the ultimate purpose of the organization and what makes us unique** among marketing companies, she educates the listener as well as promoting interest in what we do. Rather than, "An accountant, how boring," she hears, "What kind of clients do you work with at that company?" The listener is now thinking, "Who do I know that could benefit from this?"

Come up with short and direct phrases that will help people understand what the ultimate benefit will be for the customer. What is the key benefit of a cosmetic dentist? "I work with people who are interested in painlessly having one of the most attractive smiles in the world and in keeping that smile for life so they'll never be put through the pain and inconvenience of having to cope with false teeth."

Why say, "We manufacture cars," when you can say, "We deliver to our clients the most comfortable, most luxurious and safest driving machine ever designed for the American road at an incredibly reasonable price" (kind of makes you want to know what kind of car it is, doesn't it?).

Steve's wife, Cheryl, recently had their first child. When asked what she did for a living, Cheryl said proudly, "I'm a mom and housewife." But instead of people sharing her excitement about the mysteries of childbirth or the joy of decorating a new home, she was getting shelved, labelled and dismissed. Apparently she wasn't doing enough for these people!

So she changed her answer: "I've made a commitment to help correct America's most pressing social problem."

"How's that?"

"I'm ensuring that my child never ends up on your tax rolls."

Her response, because it was *different and meaningful* from the expected response, became an excellent **conversation starter,** rather than a conversation closer. Once she got them *to want to know more*, she was able to engage her listeners in non-stereotypical ways, thus changing their minds.

We call this **BOTSOM.** Change the **B**ase **O**f **T**hought by changing the **S**tate **O**f **M**ind of the person.

How do you know you're stating your Compelling Benefit Statement correctly?

When they answer, "Wow! Tell me more."

Owner's Manual

1. Make a list of all the key benefits that your company provides:

_____

_____

_____

_____

_____

2. Check off the ones that make your company compelling and unique. Practice talking about these to different people with the intention of drawing out their interest so that they ask you for more information.

The Parrot Principle

What do things go better with? Coke. Number One in car rentals? Hertz. Who tries harder? Avis. What toothpaste fights cavities? Crest. Given enough help from marketing, we'll ask for a Kleenex when we really mean a tissue or a Xerox when we really mean a copy.

Most people don't think for themselves. They've got enough to do already! They tend to repeat what is told to them. For this reason, giving an easy-to-remember Compelling Benefit Statement (CBS) is a good idea. It not only creates powerful word-of-mouth, but it helps people distinguish *this* dentist, *this* car manufacturer, *this* marketing group from all those others.

You have to watch what you tell other people because **what you say about yourself and the**

company you work for will be repeated by others—often word for word, if it's simple and catchy enough.

Privately, after a conference we'd given in Philadelphia, we described our firm to a participant as "one of the 500 fastest growing companies of its kind in the United States." Ten minutes later we overheard that very phrase used by another participant to a different group of people.

Don't assume people know what you do. Give them help.

What's the most useful thing you can do?

People learn how to talk about you by listening to how you talk about yourself.

Roger Cameron and Rene Brooks, owners of Cameron Brooks, the top Fortune 500 recruitment firm of its kind, told us they had taken this idea so seriously that they changed the way they described their company. They began calling it what it was in actuality, "a world class recruiting organization." Within weeks, people they had never met before were addressing them on the phone with that very same expression.

Use people's natural tendency to circulate information to your advantage. **Give them something to talk about that is unique and memorable, something worth repeating that places what you do in a new spot in their minds.**

Marketing is a battle of perceptions, not products.

If your message indicates that you lead or excel in a particular category, it helps a lot since no one is likely to remember an also-ran in a broad category. Better still is to narrow what you do down to a phrase that captures in the prospect's mind the essence of what your product or service does that separates you from the rest.

That's why we call our seminars *Boot Kamps*.

Owner's Manual

1. What phrase best indicates the uniqueness of what your product or service provides:

_____

_____

_____

_____

_____

2. Imagine that you could overhear the most complimentary remark about you and your company. Write down what it would be:

_____

_____

_____

_____

_____

3. Now start saying it to others!

Be Your Own Most Committed Customer

You can multiply your results with people when you really believe in what you do. And the best way to believe in the product or service your company provides is simple: **become a customer of your own organization.**

The person who speaks from the heart of experience always speaks more powerfully than the one speaking just from the head. To communicate effectively, let alone to persuade, you need to have intimate knowledge of your subject; anything short of that is hypocritical.

Have you used your own product?

If you work at a hotel, go sleep in one of the rooms; eat in the restaurant. Better to be driving the car that you sell than some other. If you work in a dental office, it's best to have your dental health attended to by the dentist with whom you work.

Everything rests on your belief.

Not only will you feel like a phony if the product or service you're involved in does not have customer value, but belief in what your company sells is the basis for the next thirty-seven ideas.

Let's put it this way: if you've used the product or service your company offers and it hasn't made you a believer, *there is no hope!* **Stop here!** Change jobs! Quickly! When you find the product or service you can believe in, go on to the next section.

Owner's Manual

1. Write down your response to using your product or service:

_____

_____

_____

_____

_____

_____

_____

_____

2. If someone very close to you—mother, spouse, sibling or best friend—were a potential customer for what your organization does, would you recommend your organization? Write down what you would say:

_____

_____

_____

_____

_____

_____

_____

_____

The Love Connection

People buy not so much because they're enthused but because you are. **They buy you first; then they buy the company you represent and the goods or services you offer.**

If they don't like you, they won't believe you. And without belief, there is no trust. And you already know how hard it is to do business without trust.

The art of persuasion requires three things: **believability, likability and trust. We call it BLT.**

The key to infectious enthusiasm is loving what you do. You know what the doctor says, "It's only work if it ain't fun." Find something you love to do because other people's interest will then be a natural consequence.

Examine the chart on the following page. We call it *the 54 multiple of human motivation.*

Notice the group at the bottom, below the 80% crowd. These are those folks whose motivation is called

The Law of the 54 Multiple
of Human Motivation

Motive to work	% of workers	Value to the company
Love To	20% of the top 20%	54x
Want To Desire To	20%	16x
NEED To	80%	1 = 1
Gotta, Oughta, Shoulda		1 < 1

gotta, oughta, shoulda. The reason that they don't even make it on to the graph is because, in terms of their value to the company, they take more than they actually give. In other words, their motivation is so poor that they are a liability to the team.

Just above them is the great mass of "employees" whose motivation rarely exceeds **need.** It's "I owe, I owe so it's off to work I go." They don't cost the company anything, but they don't add much value either.

Next is the top 20% group who **want** to go to work, those who actually **desire** to be there, the folks who would be unhappy if they didn't have the chance to go. They produce sixteen times more than everyone else.

Notice that skinny little rectangle above that. This is reserved for the 20% of the top 20% of the chart. This tiny group **loves** what they do. They produce 54 times more than everyone else.

Owner's Manual

Take this quiz. Ask yourself three questions:

• What would the customer's life be like if the product or service I'm engaged with didn't exist?

• What would the customer's life be like if the company I'm involved with didn't exist?

• What would the customer's life be like if I were not involved with the company?

If the answer to all three questions is, "Not much different," then you may not be liking what you do enough to be giving value to your job, your company and your customer. If you're not giving much value, be assured that your future is in danger. *Forget about reading this handbook! Find something you love to do first.*

When you've taken care of that, you're ready for the rest of what we have to offer. Roll up your sleeves, get out your pen, turn the page. **Let's get busy.**

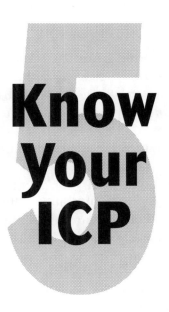

Know your ICP

Many products and services have the distinct advantage that they can be used by almost everyone, but herein lies the greatest drawback marketing-wise: if you try to be everything to everybody, you'll end up being nothing to no one.

Target your market. Do some research in one specific area: determine what your ideal customer looks. We call it identifying your ICP, that is, your Ideal Customer Profile. This way when you deal with people, you'll know when you're talking with a prime prospect. Going back to the Parrot Principle, you can also let other people know *who is the best prospect for your product or service so they can spread the word.*

Let's return to the Law of 80/20. As it is with human motivation, so it is with your business: **80% of your**

business will come from 20% of your clientele. We call it "The Best Juice with the Best Prospects." (See Chapter 2 in **Breaking the No Barrier:** *The Billion Dollar Battle Plan for Getting Everyone You Want to Say Yes to Your Proposition.* Call 800-HUNT-TEX to order.)

The largest increase in your company's business will come from the people who look, act, behave and spend like that top 20% of your client base.

What is the profile of that top 20%? You need a clear picture of who you are aiming at. And how do you find out? *You've got to ask.*

Start with someone in the sales or marketing department. If they can't describe what that top 20% customer looks like, go up a few notches to a vice president—or the president for that matter. If you still get puzzled looks, pray! It's time for some serious work on everyone's part.

If you don't know who the customer is, you just don't know what you're doing. Be in the "know." Now!

Owner's Manual

1. Describe the characteristics of your ideal customer:

_____

_____

_____

_____

Position Power With Your Prospects

Always be ready to shape whatever conversation you're in to one ultimate goal: positioning the company. The great rebounders in basketball have not all been seven foot giants. But they all have been smart players who knew where the ball was going to end up next. In a word, they have had position. Since conversations are controlled by the one who asks the questions, not the one answering them, make sure you ask.

Most of us were conditioned at a very early age to do what we are asked to do. Studies reveal that the second most popular reason people buy where they buy is *that they were asked!*

"What have you heard about our company?"

"Did you know that we have expanded our services?"

"Have you ever considered trading with us?"

These questions are simple and basic. What prevents us from asking them? Psychologists tell us that the average two-year-old child asks about fifty questions a day while a college graduate asks about two questions a day—one being, "Where's the bathroom?" So something must have happened to us while we were being educated to make us afraid of looking foolish or rejected.

We recommend what coaches repeat in the weight room: *feel the fear and do it anyway; no gain without pain.*

Since the goods and services your company provides are indeed worthwhile—or you couldn't have gotten this far in the handbook!—the pain goes away soon enough. It's only your own natural resistance to speaking up that must be overcome.

Our formula is a cinch. **Ask ten people a day to do business with you.**

Just by bringing up the topic in a casual way you'll be amazed at how people will respond. Those folks who have had some experience related to what you do may end up opening a door for your business. *Simply by positioning the company in every day conversation, you generate interest in what your company does.*

Ask and it shall be given;

    Seek and you shall find;

        Knock and it shall be opened.

THE KEY is in the **ASKing.**

Owner's Manual

1. Write down the names of the first ten people you will ask to do business with you today:

_____

_____

_____

_____

_____

Reaching Out for Repeaters

Any radio station that broadcasts over a wide area relies on repeater towers to extend the reach of the signal. Every time the signal reaches a repeater tower, it is boosted in strength and sent out to a wider area.

So who are your repeater towers? Who will help you spread the word?

The people who care about you the most.

Use your CBS and the Parrot Principle with the people who are closest to you. Start with family members. Your spouse, your children, your parents, your brothers and sisters. Make sure they understand and know how to talk about what you do, especially the key benefits of what you and your company offer, so that if they get into a conversation with someone, they could explain clearly what makes what you do unique.

In our world of acronyms, we call these people **NER: naturally existing relationships.** We say "relationship" to underline the fact that what you have with that person is a *trust and bond* that is both *mutual and reciprocal*; we describe it as "natural" meaning it's *basic* like nature, like water running in a stream; and we say "existing" meaning not a one-time deal but *continually.*

Think about all your NER's.

Now ask yourself honestly, "How many of them really know and understand what I do? Can they talk about my job and company using my Compelling Benefit Statement?"

If not, you may be selling yourself short.

Remember: Everyone talks. If you ever become the topic of a conversation (*and recognize that when a subject has common impact, it will cause people to discuss it*), you would be well served if they talked about you the way you want.

Owner's Manual

1. Make a list of all your NER's:

_____

_____

_____

_____

_____

2. Review the list. Put a check mark next to the names of all of those NER's who do not yet know how to talk about what you do.

3. Next time you talk with them, review your CBS. Make sure that they are confident that they can talk compellingly about what you do.

Extend Your Repeater Reach

Now take this list one step further. Who are the people closest to you after your immediate family, people with whom you also have a *natural existing relationship*?

Think about **who you actually talk to** on a regular basis: extended family and in-laws; new neighbors or old; members of associations you belong to at church, school or in the community; regulars at the gym, pool, golf course, park, tennis courts, health club, bowling alley, hunting and fishing club.

How about the people you know from the barber shop, beauty salon, election site, choir, folk dancing class, street or block association? Don't forget the people you run into at meetings; the various volunteer groups and advisory committees you sit on; the fraternal, civic and ethnic organizations you are a member or supporter of; your political party and its affiliates, your local councilperson or assemblyperson, Congressional and state representative.

Don't leave out those public sector people you know on a first name basis—those who serve in the police and fire departments, the clerk at the post office, the mail carrier, your local public advocate, the folks you know in sanitation and environmental control, the bus driver, train conductor, marshal, sheriff.

If you have kids, the list gets bigger. Little League, Boy and Girl Scouts, school boards, Parents Associations, related cultural programs at the library, museum, concert hall, town square, history society.

These relationships are ongoing and since you spend so much of your time at work, why not let them know what you do there in a way that they can remember and repeat to others?

Owner's Manual

1. Make a list of all these additional NER's:

_____

_____

_____

_____

_____

_____

_____

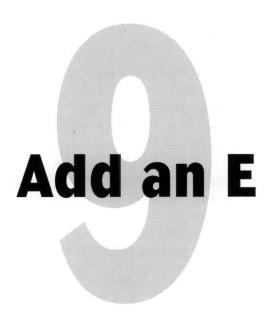

Add an E

When NER becomes NEER, we like to say you'll know the difference an E makes. **NEER** is *natural existing* **economic** *relationships*, meaning the people you pay money to for goods and services. Anyone with whom you do business, anyone to whom you write a check is in this category. Your doctor, grocer, dry cleaner, auto mechanic, accountant, dentist, clothier, landlord or mortgage company representative, real estate broker, banker, attorney, repairman, gardener, chiropractor, investor, owner of your favorite restaurant, veterinarian, computer specialist, travel consultant, therapist, stocks and bonds analyst, home improvement advisor, financial planner, nutritionist, jeweler, architect, tutor, insurance agent, decorator, masseuse, office supplier, personal trainer—among others.

Of course they want to see you do well since they are getting money from you. They succeed, to a greater or lesser extent, because of you and the money you pay them. This is what we call **a natural obligation vacuum.** *They are committed to your continued success because it means your continued use of their services.*

How is it that they may not know what your company offers?

Depending on your product or service, these NEER people are potential customers or potential word-of-mouth repeater towers. **Remember: it's much easier to get the attention of someone you're paying money to than from any other individual.**

Okay. Let's say you work in a top professional practice. Perhaps the least likely NEER prospect on that list is the guy who mows your lawn. Stop right there. If he knows your CBS, inevitably your name will come up first when he is asked whose yard he works on. Because your business gives him credibility, he will talk about you to other business prospects. Ditto down the line from the attorney to the personal trainer. It's the best advertising you are going to get. Rather than pay to spray-&-pray your Compelling Benefit Statement, NEER amounts to "riches-in-niches."

Be creative in letting people know what you do.

What's the best approach? Each situation is different. Consider the following: you walk into the dry cleaners, a place where you have been doing business for five years.

"You know, Joe Bob, I want to apologize. You've been pressing my shirts the whole time I've been living in this town. I only go to you for dry cleaning because you're fast and reliable, yet I never thought to tell you what we do out there at Canyon Springs Ranch. Today I realized how valuable the service we provide might be for you and your team. We guarantee companies like yours a 20% increase in their sales and marketing results. Could I have Joleen Jackson, who runs our business division, send you some information and give you a call? She is a first-class professional and I'll make sure she gives you the V.I.P. treatment."

Let's examine the advantages of this approach. *By beginning with an apology,* you took the weight off of Joe Bob, owner of the dry cleaners. From the first word uttered, he was "off the hook." Rather than "fish" for a compliment, a fact was stated, namely that *you rely on his professionalism.* Rather than plead with the guy for his business, you merely told him what the company you work for does. The offer you made him, which was free of any obligation, came naturally out of the service he provides. It had everything to do with friendship and reciprocity. But should Joe Bob need the service or know someone else who might, he now has an "in" along with the expectation that he'll be treated like a friend. Notice that because your name is mentioned by Joe Bob to Joleen Jackson, the head of the business division, it can only increase the perception that *you are actively adding value to the company.*

Imagine an administrative assistant at a real estate firm who encloses the company's name and key bene-fit every time he or she mails a personal check, reason-ing that at least the person who opens the envelope has to see it. It may not be the biggest thing in the life of the company, but every once in awhile someone will call having seen the enclosure—business the firm would never have had if not for the thoughtfulness of that administrative assistant's working the personal NEER.

Can you see any good business reason why you shouldn't?

Owner's Manual

1. Make a list of all your personal NEER's (go ahead, write in the margins if you need more room):

_____

_____

_____

_____

_____

_____

_____

_____

_____

_____

2. Group the NEER's according to the style of approach you will take in talking with them (three or four major categories will suffice).

3. Begin calling the easiest one in each category.

The Law of Seven Circles

Now that you've made your CBS, gotten the Parrot Principle in gear, listed your NER's and NEER's, return to your ICP.

Identify all those individuals in the community that you would like to meet, people who might fit that profile as ideal customers. **The Law of Seven Circles says that you're only seven people away from knowing everyone in the world.**

More often than not, you will already have people in your own sphere of influence who can reach out and, if not touch them directly, at least put you in touch with someone who can.

It's fewer than seven phone calls away. The trick is to be willing to ask, "Do you know anyone who knows Mr. Ideal Customer?"

Let us give an example which happened recently at one of our Boot Kamps. A young woman came to us with outstanding grades as an undergraduate, a high score on the LSAT and a host of exceptional personal recommendations. As the seminar continued, participants were struck by how bright and supportive she was. When it was her turn to tell the group how she intended to apply the training she was getting at Boot Kamp, she told us she wanted to go to Vanderbilt Law School. Although she qualified in every way, she knew she was one of thousands of hopefuls competing for only a limited number of seats. She had no leverage beyond her remarkable track record as a student. Spontaneously, hands went up. One participant, a man from New Jersey who had done very well in law, had been a graduate of Vanderbilt. He remained in close contact with one of the professors there. Another participant knew the former governor of Tennessee who was a close friend of the Law School Dean. A third participant was married to someone who served on one of Vanderbilt's alumni committees.

When this happens over and over again, it confirms our belief that there are no accidents, that chance has perhaps some inner logic. More significant, however, than even that "unlikely" Vanderbilt contingent, was the degree to which everyone present had wanted to help her.

Eliminate the idea that successful and influential people don't want to know you or help you. That's why those people are influential in the first place. They work at it.

We all secretly think that people we hold in high esteem really don't want to be introduced to little ol' us. Instead of respect and admiration being reasons

NOT to make someone's acquaintance, reconsider; *respect and admiration may be the ONLY reasons to meet someone.*

Owner's Manual

1. Make a list of all the people in your community that you would like to meet because they would be ideal customers or influencers for your business:

_____

_____

_____

_____

_____

_____

_____

_____

_____

_____

_____

_____

_____

_____

2. Next to each name write down all the people you know who might know that person or who might know someone who knows them.

The Sphere of 250

If you add up all your NER's and NEER's, the average number of people you are likely to interact with and influence, directly or indirectly, is about 250 folks. That's the estimate, social scientists tell us, of how far the average person reaches.

Not a very large number when you think about it.

But what makes all the difference in the world is that this number will expand exponentially!

Every member of your sphere of 250 each has a sphere of 250!

In other words, if each person in your sphere of 250 were to carry your message to their individual sphere of 250 you would have reached 62,500 people. Now that's getting the message out! Furthermore, don't forget that every *new* person that you meet—whether a customer, prospect, supplier, vendor, friend or relation—also has a sphere of influence of about 250 people.

This is the second part of the Law of the Seven Circles. And what is its value to you?

When you introduce yourself to anyone— a new client, prospect, co-worker, associate or friend—imagine 250 people standing outside the door. Because that's how many people that person is likely to influence—directly or indirectly.

Owner's Manual

1. List the last three people you met recently in any situation—party, formal gathering or just on the street. Based on what you know about them, who might they know who could be a prospect or an influencer for your organization:

_____

_____

_____

_____

_____

_____

_____

Opening Up the "Help Line"

As we discussed in the Law of Seven Circles, **asking people for their help is a form of flattery.** If you approach those you admire and respect with BLT, they will feel it. *People like to be admired and respected.*

To ask someone's opinion on an issue you're already excited about, namely prospects for your goods and services, is a compliment. It means that you honor their wisdom, insight, judgment and basic business acumen.

"If you were I and you worked for a company like I work for, what would you be doing to get the word out?"

It's great when all of your NER and NEER people are thinking about potential customers for you.

"I work for a great organization and this is the compelling benefit that we provide our customers. Who do you know that you think might have a need or an interest in what we offer?"

But let's imagine a worst case scenario. Let's say you hate looking unprofessional, like the lawyer who chases ambulances because it's the only work he or she can get. Ideas about prestige may have boxed you into a corner so that by even appearing to be on the look-out for more clients you fear you may be thought of as a hustler, thereby losing your perceived superiority in the marketplace.

Say one simple thing: "I'm working for a rapidly expanding company that is always looking for good quality customers who appreciate the value of the product and service we provide."

Let's resolve another mistaken notion about what is wrongly called "tooting your own horn." Let's say you're a medical doctor, a cancer specialist, and you happen to have a close friend of yours who becomes ill. Before your friend is diagnosed as having terminal cancer, you probably have noted all the tell-tale signs. Wouldn't you tell your friend what you see? Let's put it this way: if you didn't, your friend would probably think it was pretty strange should they find out later that all of the signs of cancer were present and you said nothing.

So it goes with the product or service you offer. Always be on the look-out and let it be known.

Owner's Manual

1. Consider that everyone you deal with outside the company is a potential customer.

2. If you know you provide something which is a great benefit for people, you'd better be telling them!

Speak Out

There has been more information produced in the last 30 years than during the previous 5,000. **The information supply available to us doubles every five years.** The Industrial Age has given way to the Information Age.

Whether you are in the sales department or not, being able to speak in public is becoming an increasingly valuable skill. The biggest job companies face today is not so much in *selling* as it is in *educating* their client base.

Every organization that exists—from the PTA to the local Knights of Columbus—is looking for interesting speakers. Whatever expertise you have, there is a way to make this of interest to other people.

Join Toastmasters. This local group will give you weekly opportunities to practice speaking in front of others. **The secret to success in speaking in front of**

people is to find a topic you love and position yourself as an expert in that field. Make sure that you can speak from personal experience. The best way to give a speech is to illustrate it with examples from your own life.

What can this skill in public speaking do for you? In terms of getting your product or service known in the community, the sky is literally the limit!

By speaking regularly, your name and face become better and better known.

Your profile—and that of the company—will be raised. And practice does make perfect. Your communication skills will necessarily become more honed as well.

The more you speak, the more effective a speaker you become.

(Call 800-HUNT-TEX for our audio cassette program, **Speak and the Money Will Follow:** *The No Fear Guide to Promoting Your Business and Yourself Through the Power of Public Speaking*, our collaboration with Bill Gove, Founder of the National Speakers Association.)

Another advantage is what we call **chumming.**

By that we mean that people, especially if your CBS strikes curiosity in their minds, will seek you out. Everyone is looking for a speaker—Lions, Kiwanis, Rotary, Women's Auxiliary, Junior League—and all you have to do is make yourself available.

Owner's Manual

1. Write down the three or four topics that you are most knowledgeable about, topics that you have plenty of personal experience to draw from, topics that you would like to speak on for fifteen to twenty minutes:

_____

_____

_____

_____

_____

_____

_____

2. What kind of groups that exist in your town would be interested in your expertise:

_____

_____

_____

_____

_____

_____

_____

Be a Spark Plug

So far, all of the concepts we have been discussing relate to what you do with people OUTSIDE the organization. **Consider how your value to the company can increase when you share these ideas within the company.**

Be the spark plug in your organization by helping motivate co-workers on your team.

Imagine what happens when CBS, ICP, Sphere of 250, BLT, NER's and NEER's become part of the vocabulary of the workplace. Having shared these ideas—and what you're doing with them—with other company members will invariably cause you to be seen as a source and a resource, a center of influence, within the company itself.

Donna B. Blue, who runs our Eagle University Young Adult Seminars and one of our best "idea people," often shares her success stories with other team members. She never misses an opportunity to talk about Planned

Marketing with people she meets. She will come in on a Monday morning and recount a conversation she started on an airplane or at a party, a conversation which led to that new person becoming a customer.

Her example and her sharing it with others gives team members courage and confidence to do the same. When they do, Donna is the first one to recognize them in front of the rest of the company. She's a real spark plug, someone who gets everyone else going on all cylinders.

The idea needn't be the most original one in the world but when shared within the company it can improve others' lives as well as your own.

Owner's Manual

1. What success stories can you share with your team members to make the environment you work in a more productive place:

_____

_____

_____

_____

2. What other team members can you brag on to the rest of the team:

_____

_____

_____

_____

Filling the Obligation Vacuums

Depending on where you work in the organization, suggest or create a dialogue with the people to whom your company pays money. Make sure that your accounts payable understand that they have an opportunity to be partners with you and help participate in the company's growth.

NEER common sense tells you that the vendor should know what goods and services—and what key benefits—the company provides. In addition, the vendor had better know where you're going and the kind of customer for whom you're looking.

Make an unmistakable invitation to the vendor to help bring in new customers.

It's a natural obligation vacuum. In fact, since they are already benefitting from your business, they ought to be giving you something back in return.

When and how to approach them is a *matter of practical observation*. Wanda, our purchasing manager, deals with suppliers all day. But when she's buying, she looks for opportunities to sell as well. She first determines the interests and needs of the vendor.

Some time ago, she had noticed that one of the companies from whom we buy office supplies had trouble keeping sales representatives. When the sales manager arrived one day, accompanied by a new sales rep, she pulled the manager aside.

"Susan, we've been doing business for a few years now. Am I right in observing that you seem to have a lot of turnover in your sales department?"

"Yes, Wanda, we can't seem to get them to stay."

"Did you know that one of the services we're most proud of providing to our customers is sales training?"

"I wasn't aware of that."

"Did you know that our trainers are so confident of our program's effectiveness that if you don't see a 20% increase in sales, we'll refund the money?"

"No kidding."

"Can I have someone from our client services department give you a call?"

Wanda informed Susan of what she wanted to know. Wanda didn't push, so Susan had no reason to be defensive. Wanda eliminated the only embarrassing circumstance by pulling Susan aside to discuss a problem that would have been inappropriate in front of the new sales rep. Notice how Wanda spoke to Susan. She didn't *tell* so much as *engage Susan each time with a question*. This allowed Wanda to evaluate Susan's level of interest and not waste her time. And since Wanda informed her of a service that she could use, Susan probably was grateful. She was never under any obligation to buy anything.

Wanda followed one important guideline. We call it **KIS/MIF: keep it simple, make it fun.**

In terms of the likelihood of a sale, Wanda's sales team could not be happier. The potential customer is already "pre-heated"—taking the cold out of the call.

Owner's Manual

1. Make a list of the people your company pays money to for goods or services:

_____

_____

_____

_____

_____

2. Who in your company, if not you, can most favorably reach out to each of the individuals listed above?

_____

_____

_____

_____

_____

"Leave the Gate Open"

When you're having a conversation with a customer, it makes sense, just in the course of things, to leave the gate open for new business. Say, for example: "Have you ever told anyone about what our company has been able to do for you?" Or: "When was the last time you spoke to someone about what has happened since we started working together?" Or: "I know you do business with a lot of people throughout your day. When the opportunity arises to talk about what we do together, I'd sure like those people to know that I'm ready to give them the same V.I.P. treatment as I give you."

Often, given the opportunity, they will say, "Yeah, I'd been meaning to tell you about that. I've spoken to a number of people."

Sometimes just by making satisfied customers aware that you are looking for other customers **just**

like them they will, *as an act of courtesy and an expression of gratitude*, help you out.

People like you more when they're helping you than when you're helping them.

It all begins with your willingness to open the door to dialogue. For a great many satisfied customers, referring other customers to you is a pleasure.

Owner's Manual

1. List your favorite and most satisfied customers:

_____

_____

_____

_____

_____

2. How will you reach them with the news that you're looking for other customers just like them?

_____

_____

_____

_____

_____

Give Yourself Away

Everyone needs something outside of work that they enjoy doing, something that makes them feel better about themselves while doing it. An avocation or hobby is, by definition, not work; it's fun, the highest form of play. Whether it's volunteering at the local ambulance corps, camping with the Scouts, playing chess or bridge, golfing at the country club, becoming a Big Brother or Sister, collecting stamps and coins, researching the Civil War, coaching basketball at the local Y or joining the Adult Education Center, if it has to do with people, make it work for the company as well. How?

Become your company's representative in local organizations. What do you mean you can't? You already love what you're doing both with the company and with your volunteer organization. So find a prominent position. Why just participate when you could get really involved? It's easier than you think and the position is probably already waiting for you.

Take on one of the two most unwanted jobs: the membership committee chair or the fund raiser chair.

Why are these jobs unwanted? Because they are hard to do without a NER and NEER network. With what you have learned already from this handbook, not only will you do well in either of these positions with your systematic approach, but you will garner a great deal of **exposure and prestige.** Furthermore, *you will meet more people in either of these capacities than in any others.*

You needn't start with the White House Children's Defense Fund, a cure for cancer or Farm Aid. Start smaller and discover how, with a degree of planning and an eye for bringing new business to your company, it can teach you more and more about becoming an effective communicator and a persuader.

Owner's Manual

1. List every volunteer group and public service work with which you are involved:

_____

_____

_____

_____

_____

_____

2. How can you leverage your company's best interests in each of these organizations:

_____

_____

_____

_____

_____

_____

"Collecting All Cards"

Don't give out cards. Collect them instead.

Why give away *your* business cards when you could collect *their* business cards? What is the psychology of handing out your card to people? What happens when you give your card away?

Consider that **he or she who has the other's business card is in a position to control the next step of the relationship.**

Don't think of this exclusively as a power play. You have their card. You know what they are looking for and where they are located. You can send them things that you think they would be interested in. You can be on the look-out for what they need. You can network what they are doing with all of what you are doing. And you can follow up immediately.

Collect more than you give.

If you have given your card away and have received nothing in return, you are doing something wrong.

Owner's Manual

1. Centralize all the business cards ever given to you in one place. Organize it with a roll-a-dex or notebook so that it's easy to flip through them.

2. Get in the habit of reviewing these cards periodically. Ask yourself if you know what the person behind the card really wants and needs. Be on the look-out for ways to serve them.

Two By Two Leverage

Find out who does what you do in other companies in your community, companies that do not compete with the goods and services your company offers.

The first value of this information is professional. It's good thinking for people who do the same function in the community to be associated with each other. An accountant ought to know all the other accountants in the area. This is a smart move career-wise, but it also sets up a network of peers who can help keep one another updated on developments within your field.

For our purposes it's particularly wise because **it puts you in touch with so many people who not only are prospects themselves for the goods and services your company may offer, but who also interact with so many people they can stay on the look-out for other prospects for you.**

If your profession already has an association, it's a great idea to join. Finding and getting to know your peers has an additional value as well which the next section will presently point out.

Owner's Manual

1. List as many companies in your community as you can think of, companies that offer goods and services unlike your own:

_____

_____

_____

_____

_____

2. How many of the people do you know in these companies who do what you do? Next to the company listed, write in their names.

3. What is preventing you from joining—or starting—an organization of peer professionals?

The Never Ending Search

How do you become perceived as a resource for your company? **Be the source for bringing well qualified, new team members into the company.**

85% of the jobs that people find do not come from the classified ads in newspapers and magazines, nor do they come from job placement services. They come from word-of-mouth from existing team members.

Take the limelight. Bring a star on board the company.

The very best recruitment idea is always to be aware of people who might be good for your company.

Owner's Manual

1. Find out the kind of professional your company needs.

Where do you find such a person? Everywhere you do business, all your NER's and NEER's, all those people you talk to about what your company does.

2. Find out what they do and what their skills are as well as their qualities and personal characteristics.

3. Ask yourself if such a person would fit in well with what your organization is looking for in that position.

4. Be careful not to be so enthusiastic that you appear like a head hunter. Follow these guidelines:

- If the person you're talking with *already* has a job, don't try to talk them into leaving and joining up with your outfit. Be thoughtful enough to say, "Our company is looking for someone *just like you*. Let me know if you might know of anyone who might be interested."

- If the person is truly unhappy with the company he or she is working for, then it's **up to him or her** to come forward. Having made the invitation known, you have done all that is necessary.

Find a Partne(e)r

Go back to your Owner's Manual for peer professionals that follows Idea #19. Review the list of all the companies who call on, or sell to, the same target market as your company does, BUT who don't compete with the goods and services you provide.

Meet the people in those other companies. Why? **They are a free sales force for you.**

They're an ultimate source of referrals. They will naturally come across people in their target market who need what your company provides. We call this **PART-NEERing.**

The three criteria for a PART-NEER are:

1. *they provide a value for their customer;*

2. *they do it with integrity;*

3. *they do not compete with what you do.*

Do you think it's difficult to figure out a way to make their acquaintance?

"I heard about you and what you do. We really like the service your company provides. We run into a lot of people. In fact, many of our customers could benefit from your service. We'd like to send them your way. I also want to introduce to you the product we provide so that if you run into any of your customers who could benefit from it, we'd appreciate their business as well."

Owner's Manual

1. Form an association with your very best PART-NEER's.

2. Grow your group cautiously. Don't go out and sign up the first fifteen people who are dying to come to a meeting. The process is not easy.

3. Let two members decide on a third, three members decide on a fourth until you have culled the most qualified professionals in your community who have the same target market as you as well as the same commitment, are not competitors and whose collective mind power works harmoniously to bring greater business to all. What does it spell? **P**rofessional **A**dvisory **R**esearch **T**eam **N**etworking **E**xisting **E**conomic **R**elationships.

Bear Good News

People have an interest in primarily two things: what is new and what is different. *People don't like to be bored.* Even when you run into someone you haven't seen for a long time, the topic of conversation generally focuses on what is new and what you both are doing now that is different from before.

Always be aware of what is going on in your organization that is new and different.

Though this would seem to apply more for new customers and prospects, it's *doubly valuable for existing customers.* Often customers will change the place they do business for no other reason than that they are bored. They want something new and exciting. *Become responsible for creating compelling word-of-mouth.*

Be the person who stays up on what everyone in the organization is doing. **Coordinate and circulate** the good news—on the telephone, in the hallways, during meetings.

"Tell me what's new."

This way every time you speak with a peer, customer or prospect, you're helping to create an impression because **every impression is an opportunity for another sale.**

Always having good things to say about the company sends many messages:

    —*the company has ability;*

    —*people in the company share their good fortune;*

    —*you've got loyalty to the company.*

These three perceptions say an awful lot.

But beyond the tremendous impact that talking up the company can do for the customer, don't forget the impact it can have on the other members of your team.

Owner's Manual

1. What will you have to do to become the most informed person in your company about what it is doing that is new and different:

_____

_____

_____

_____

_____

"PEP" Squad (Promote Every Partner)

Bragging about your team is a piggy-back idea to the Good News principle. When someone in your organization has done something worthy of note, tell people about it. Let people know how smart, innovative and creative the members of your team have proven to be.

Stay informed about what people do in order to share their success with others.

Let's say you work in accounts receivable. A customer calls wanting information about his or her bill. You take care of the problem expeditiously. Generally, what happens next is that the customer thanks you and hangs up. But imagine the conversation continuing.

In the same tone of helpfulness, you might add: "Have you heard that the head of our company has just received an award for top business person of the year?"

Strictly speaking, the customer didn't ask to know the additional information, but bragging on your boss's accomplishment, especially in his or her absence, is a great strategy. You can say things that your boss could never say without running the risk of sounding conceited. It's not pushy and you didn't gush; you only informed.

You have done your company a service, even if the customer doesn't do more business immediately as a result.

You have dressed up your company. You are doing the whole team a load of good just by talking the talk. And having the mentality of "what else is this person a prospect for?" will help keep the opportunities flowing.

The best thing you can do for the company is to be on the look-out for other things you might mention to a customer whenever you have occasion to talk to one.

That means knowing what the people around you are doing. Start a weekly brag sheet. Post it on a bulletin board or circulate a flyer. Get every member of your team thinking that their accomplishments are not simply personal triumphs but greater opportunities to sell the company's goods and services.

"Has anyone told you that our Kimberly just received the state award for sales last month?"

"Did you know that Hailey was just voted into the Texas Music Hall of Fame?"

"I'm sure you've heard that our service department just won its second consecutive national award for quality."

Always have good things to say about the company, especially when a potential customer is likely to **overhear** you. Bragging on your sales force or accounting group or management team deepens that message of loyalty, team work and can-do-ness. You'll notice, in addition, that **praise works wonders for the sense of hearing.**

Owner's Manual

1. Make a list of every person or department in your company:

_____

_____

_____

_____

_____

_____

_____

_____

_____

_____

_____

_____

2. Next to the name of the person or department, write their latest accomplishment. If you don't know it, find out. If you do know, make them aware that you do. Send a note.

Spread the Good News About your Customers

Let your customers know about the success you have had with other customers—how satisfied they were, what a good experience they had.

Staying informed of the success of your customers and finding opportunities to brag on them does two things for the existing or prospective customer: *it reassures their faith in your long-term ability to perform and it will keep them coming back.*

The best customer to have is the one who is not only a prime buyer but a prime influencer. Take notice of the customer whose decisions will be watched—and followed—by others.

Let's say a customer calls with a question about a service.

"Interesting that you should ask about that, Mr. Jones. I've just finished talking with John Williams over at ABC Widgets, the largest widget company in town, who started using our service a few months ago. He called to say our service is saving them a tremendous amount of money."

If the information on your customer is confidential, particularly when you are speaking with a competitor of that customer, use a more general approach. You needn't overstate your point. And the point is this:

People look for validation on their business decisions. The more reassurance you can provide from your own experience and the experience of your satisfied customers, the more it helps your new customer make the right decision. Taking an interest in your customer's success is a WIN WIN situation—their success can help you succeed with other customers.

Owner's Manual

1. Don't just keep a file on the testimonials your satisfied customers send you. Copy them, circulate them, talk about them.

Become a Creative (Re)Source for Good Ideas

To become a source and resource of good ideas takes a real commitment. It begins with a priority to be a learner, to take the personal responsibility to be always seeking out ideas that will be *value-added* to other people—customers, prospects, NER's or NEER's.

There is no better reputation to have.

Every time they speak on the telephone or sit down with you, they know you will have something of value that will enrich their lives. They will always look forward to seeing you because *they know you have something that will help them.*

No matter what you do within your organization, if you resolve that every time you contact someone outside the organization you will provide valuable ideas, then you are adding a tremendous plus to the marketing success of your firm.

Before the members of our team start their week, they've reviewed and discussed a new idea that morning. It might be something related to business, finance or personal growth. Whether they sell something to their prospects or are just talking with a customer, they say: "Before I let you off the phone, let me share with you a neat little idea that might help you out with what you're doing."

Owner's Manual

1. Organize your information. Make sure you have something of value to give anyone who happens to call you.

2. Never let a phone call become run-of-the-mill. Make sure the transaction always ends with something that could enhance the customer's life.

A Gatherer & a Sower Be

Do *inside* the company what you have learned to do *outside* the company with Idea #25.

Gain the reputation within your firm as a value-adder. Become viewed as someone who is a go-to resource, a person who is always growing, someone whose brain works, someone able to come up with great ideas. No matter what department you're in, make sure the folks down the hall in accounting or in shipping and receiving or in the service department know that *you are not afraid to share ideas with them.*

"I ran across this article. I thought it might be of interest to you. I hope you enjoy it."

Notice that in being direct and humble, you take the ego out of the interaction. If your suggestion is perceived as a power play, it will backfire. The last thing co-workers want to deal with is a bratty know-it-all.

That's why we say: **Be interested, not interesting.**

Owner's Manual

1. Change your job description so that it includes looking at the company as something to which you're committed to adding value.

2. Become, for all practical purposes, a consultant to your team. Be on the look-out for ideas and resources that will help other team members.

Fill Your Shoes & Find Some New Ones

If you think you're not replaceable, then you've taken the first step toward extinction. **The fastest way to lose your job is to think that you're indispensable.** Why?

Any organization that has someone in it who has positioned him or herself as being irreplaceable, either because he or she has information that no one else has or a skill that no one else can do, is the greatest threat to a firm's success. Leadership knows that such a person has the power to endanger the organization should he or she decide to leave the firm, and rather than be compelled to tolerate the whims of that person, leadership would sooner replace him or her.

Owner's Manual

1. Commit to improve your position always, of finding better ways to do what you do for the company.

2. Always be asking yourself who in the organization is going to replace you when you move to the next level, who you're training to take your place.

Be a Private I

We're all consumers. *We all make buying decisions constantly.* Anytime you find yourself in a position either to make a purchase or observe others making a purchase, become a private eye. **Log positive and negative experiences.**

Notice everything—how the salesperson talks to you, how effective the display is in attracting your interest, how willing the company you're buying from is to go that extra mile. If they are doing something useful, intelligent and customer-conscious, bring it to the attention of the right department in your organization. If they are doing something harmful to the customer or are just thoughtless, make sure that your company is wise to avoid that.

This is also a great source of good ideas for prospects and clients as well.

Owner's Manual

1. Wherever you are, it's good policy to ask: **how can what they are doing be applied to what we are doing?**

"All I Know Is What I Read in the Papers"

Will Rogers said it first a long while ago, and we still like the sound of it. We want to go one better and suggest to you to quit reading the newspaper for news. If you want to know if there's a catastrophe nearby, a neighbor will be kind enough to tell you. The newspaper has a much better function. Use it every day to build your business.

- **Read the paper like a public relations person might**—with an eye toward helping to inform and inspire the people with whom you work.

  Where do you find such a person? Everywhere you do business, all your NER's and NEER's, all those people you talk to about what your company does.

- **Get out that red felt tip pen** and begin to circle anything of interest for the company or the client, anything that can create an opportunity:

- ► *What names are mentioned in the business section?*
- ► *What names and faces appear on the society page? and in the gossip columns?*
- ► *What movers and shakers are featured in the metro section?*
- ► *What projects are they working on?*
- Ask yourself: **is this person a potential PARTNEER, a potential customer, a good resource to know?** Who do you know who needs to know what they are doing?
- Don't just cut out the article and send it to the people who could use the information. **Laminate the article. Staple your card in the upper right hand corner.** This way you make a lasting impression.

Owner's Manual

1. *Take that red felt tip pen* to breakfast tomorrow morning. Instead of reading the paper for news, read it for prospects.

YES! Send Me

☐ Information on Planned Marketing's Boot Kamp Seminars **FREE**

☐ Information on Eagle University for Young Adults **FREE**

☐ The Everybody Search Plan **$12.95**

☐ Breaking the No Barrier **$15.95**

☐ How to Form a MasterMind Alliance **$9.95**

☐ Speak and the Money Will Follow Audio Series **$39.95**
(Please add $4.95 shipping for every two books)

Name _____ Phone (w/area code) _____

Shipping Address _____

City / State / Zip _____

Signature _____

Credit card number _____ ☐ Visa ☐ Mastercard ☐ AmEx Exp. Date _____

Call 800·HUNT·TEX
PLANNED MARKETING A S S O C I A T E S

Keep Up with Our Proven Marketing Techniques

☐ **YES!** I am interested in more information on Planned Marketing's Boot Kamp Seminars and other marketing books and products.

Name _____ Phone (w/area code) _____

Shipping Address _____

City / State / Zip _____

PLANNED MARKETING A S S O C I A T E S

For our FREE catalog call 800·HUNT·TEX

BUSINESS REPLY MAIL
FIRST-CLASS MAIL PERMIT NO. 300 HUNT TX

POSTAGE WILL BE PAID BY THE ADDRESSEE

Planned Marketing, Inc.
Publications Division
P.O. Box 345
Hunt TX 78024-9978

BUSINESS REPLY MAIL
FIRST-CLASS MAIL PERMIT NO. 300 HUNT TX

POSTAGE WILL BE PAID BY THE ADDRESSEE

Planned Marketing, Inc.
Publications Division
P.O. Box 345
Hunt TX 78024-9978

Help Me Count the Ways We Can Help

No matter where you work, any time you come in contact with a customer you should say to them:

- "We really appreciate your business. Is there anything else we can do for you that we're not already doing?"

- "Is there anything that will serve your needs better?"

- "Is there anything that we could do to make you more comfortable?"

The research on why people stop being customers reveals that the single greatest reason is the quality of the interaction. **68% of all customers quit because they are treated poorly.**

So expressing appreciation and showing you care can add tremendous value.

Owner's Manual

1. From time to time, just call the customers you deal with for no other reason than to show appreciation. **This raises you above the competition and positions you as a source and resource within the company to that particular customer. They'll never forget it.**

I Hear You, But How Do You Really Feel?

Any time you interact with a customer who has had an experience with what your company provides, **ask them for performance feedback.**

- "In what ways does our service match up—or fail to match up—with what you were looking for?"

- "How could we improve our responsiveness to you as a client?"

- "How do you like our product?"

The reasons to ask these simple questions are many. For starters, *very few companies ever ask the customer anything.*

Just by asking, you distinguish yourself and your company. But in addition, asking them for their experience with your product or service lets the listener know:

- *that you care about them;*
- *that their opinion actually matters to you;*
- *that sincerity has been offered, a gesture toward a friendlier relationship has been made;*
- *that you're involved with what you do, that you believe in the company and what it delivers;*
- *that you welcome an honest and direct response.*

In addition, the feedback itself is always useful—either in telling you more about the customer or in letting you know how the actual goods and services you provide could be enhanced. Furthermore, by being interested in what they have to say, you open the door for the next level of relationship.

It's much easier to ask for a referral or a testimonial after you have discovered what they like about what your company does.

Owner's Manual

1. Take the first step. Make sure you ASK for feedback every time you talk with a customer.

The Million Dollar Phone Call

Never pass judgment on the value of a customer.

Treat every customer as if he or she were worth a million dollars to the company. Why? Because you just can't overestimate a customer's long-term value! A satisfied customer will most certainly speak to someone about the pleasure of doing business with you or the quality of the goods or services they purchased from you. Statistics tell us:

- **the average satisfied customer will tell 1.5 to 2 people** about his or her good experience. However,

- **the average dissatisfied customer will tell at least 9 people** about his or her bad experience! Moreover,

- **at least 13% of the dissatisfied will tell over 20 people.**

Tough numbers, huh? The value of this research for our purposes is simply that you can't afford to dismiss anyone or allow personal prejudice to overcome your better judgment. Just remember the next time the phone rings: **Courtesy is the only solution.** Additionally, it's wise to **think of the customer in terms of a lifetime.**

How do you determine the average value of any customer?

Multiply what he or she buys in a year times the number of years you do business with that customer. The local dry cleaners, for example, is not a business you would think as having a very high average. When was the last time you paid more than thirty or forty dollars when you picked up your dry cleaning? However, if you use their service only once every two weeks, your monthly expense might be as high as fifty dollars. In a year that's $600. In ten years, an average lifetime for a customer, that number becomes $6,000. Were you to be treated so well that you told just two other friends or neighbors who then decided to use that same dry cleaners, that lifetime number could become as high as $18,000.

That simple $30 transaction now takes on new meaning.

The value of all this math is to help everyone on the team to remember to **share in the responsibility of keeping the customer for a lifetime.** Furthermore, it's from existing customers that a good deal of your business will come.

Owner's Manual

1. Following the format on the previous page, calculate the average value of a new customer in your business. Who can you share this information with inside the company? Who would benefit from this information the most? Do it.

_____

_____

_____

_____

_____

_____

_____

_____

_____

_____

_____

Think
BESA

Research tells us that it's **80% easier to make the second sale than the first.**

The biggest expense a company has is in creating a first-time customer. That's where most of the time and money goes. Add value to the company and to your job by identifying BESA: **B**ack **E**nd **S**ales **A**nnuity.

Always take the opportunity with the people you serve to let them know about the new products and services that you offer. Existing customers are the best prospects for *other* goods and services that your company provides.

"I know you are happy with Product X, but have you heard about our new line of Y and Z?"

Keeping customers aware of other products and services you offer also lets them spread the word to other prospective customers.

Owner's Manual

1. Which customers have you talked to during the last week who may not be aware of "what's new?"

_____

_____

_____

_____

_____

_____

_____

_____

1. Who will you be talking to next week who might benefit from "what's new?"

_____

_____

_____

_____

_____

_____

_____

_____

Be a Pain Reliever, Not Just a Problem Solver

The best way to create a lifetime customer is to find out where their deepest pain is—and help them solve it, even if it is not related to the goods and services you provide.

Your job should be to help people solve their TOTAL problem, not just the problem your company was set up to solve.

What do you know about the customer?
How long has he or she been in town?
How long employed at the firm he or she now works at?
Been promoted? Thinking of switching careers?
Married? Happily? With children?
How old are the kids? How are they doing in school?
*   Plans for college?*

These are not questions to interrogate your customer with so much as the natural topics that will come up over time. Showing an interest in the rest of the life

OUTSIDE the services you provide **gives customers permission to discuss what's getting in their way.**

Moreover, whenever you can provide something that will assist them in moving toward the bigger picture, then **you will have created an emotional bond that is many times stronger than just an economic relationship.**

You don't have to be a psychotherapist, marriage counselor or match-maker either. Sometimes it's as easy as helping a client who has relocated from another city with introductions to the right circle of people in the new town.

Owner's Manual

1. Actively work to help clients out in ALL aspects of their lives.

2. This will increase the likelihood of a longer term relationship with your organization. **When they know that you understand what they really want, they'll be more likely to stay loyal because they have a true relationship with you.**

Spread Cheer, Not FEAR

The best ideas come from groups of people who are relaxed enough to let their imaginations take them over. People cannot work together effectively when individuals are afraid. They will be neither productive nor creative.

Only where fear has been eliminated, replaced by an atmosphere of harmony and trust, can the most creative ideas flourish.

Remove the sense of FEAR, what we call **F**alse **E**vidence **A**ppearing **R**eal. Particularly when it comes to opening up to share ideas, that's often all that fear really is: he won't like what I say; she'll think I'm stupid; they don't want to hear from me; what if I'm not as smart? *Et cetera, ad nauseam.*

Owner's Manual

1. Take responsibility for making the place you work an environment of harmony and trust so that new ideas can really happen.

2. Enhance your value by becoming known as a center of harmony and trust within your organization, where customers and co-workers like to come, where potential solutions to problems will get heard.

3. Develop the reputation not just as a creative problem solver, but as someone who creates a *resistance-free zone for other people's ideas.*

4. Help generate and support the problem-solving skills of the people around you.

5. Treat your co-workers with the same respect and attention as you would your best and most valued customer.

Inside
Master Mind

Ideally, a company should be a Master Mind alliance, that is, *a collection of two or more individuals working in harmony for the attainment of a definite objective*. Unlike the association of PARTNEER's described in Idea #21 whose focus is *narrow* (namely helping one another find prospects), the idea behind the Master Mind is more *open-ended*.

Picture it as an ultimate think tank.

By joining forces with other people, people you trust, respect and admire, you expand your company's problem-solving skills immeasurably. In fact, that's what Master Minding is all about—meeting with the most intelligent people you can find, people from diverse backgrounds, who bring to the brainstorming table different sets of assets. Mixing and matching ideas, working universal principles into new configurations, linking up what worked for someone else and seeing how to apply their success to your project's success, you arrive at solutions you never would have figured out by yourself.

When two or more minds are joined in harmony, **an additional mind is formed,** *one only limited by the ability of those minds to work together to achieve a common purpose* (for more information, see **How to Form a Master Mind Alliance:** *Coordinate Knowledge & Effort in a Spirit of Harmony to Multiply Your Effectiveness and Produce Richer Results.* Call 1-800-HUNT-TEX to order).

Owner's Manual

1. Create this level of interaction with people *inside* the company. You will multiply your value to the firm. Not only are you now giving the best that you've got, but you are in a Master Mind alliance that draws like a magnet the best out of the other members of your team.

Be a Transitional Thinker

Reflecting on the history of ideas reveals that only 10% of any idea is actually "new." Since Solomon has already said, "There's nothing new under the sun," it might be wise of us to say **there may be no new ideas, only new connections of ideas.** Which invention has had more impact:

- *the airplane or the jet engine?*

- *the radio or the transistor?*

- *the telephone or the electronic switching system?*

- *the computer or the computer chip?*

In all four cases, though the first choice may have been the more revolutionary invention, the second choice proved to revolutionize more lives.

There are very few people who deal in what is called pure creativity and those that do come up with things like the Theory of Relativity. Fortunately, the solution to most every day problems in business has much more to do with re-thinking what we already know.

What is needed is not so much a pure thinker as a transitional thinker, a person capable of sync-ing and linking, that is, listening to the input of other people and applying their ideas in a new configuration.

Think of it this way: *the best ideas are only 10% new.*

Better still: *a 10% improvement may yield a 100% return.* When the Worchestershire Sauce Company couldn't figure out how to increase their sales, they finally asked the team members of the firm for their opinions. The solution: make the bottle's neck wider so that when you turn the bottle over and pour, more sauce comes out. It put them over the top. Who thought up the answer? The janitor.

Owner's Manual

1. Get in the habit of asking: what are the add-ons to the already good ideas our company is using? **How can their idea become our idea?**

2. Bring to your customers and prospects new applications of strategies which have already proven effective but in different contexts. We like to say, **why create mediocrity when you can copy genius?**

3. Find a problem you can't solve. Like the detective in a mystery, don't rest until you put the case to bed first. Unlike Sam Spade, however, link up your separate minds to create a more powerful collective mind. **When transitional thinkers create a Master Mind alliance, you've got one of the most powerful forces in the universe at your disposal.**

Outside Master Mind

Sometimes the best ideas, professionally and personally, will come from someone completely outside the industry you work in. Even the brightest minds are dulled by repetition. Bringing new blood on board, people in different career tracks in different industries, sometimes can create the greatest benefit. They see the obvious things that insiders miss. **That's why forming your own Master Mind group is the smartest decision you can make for your long term future.**

Owner's Manual

1. Using the description outlined in Idea #36, join forces with eight to twelve people in your community whose ideas are sound and whose impulses you trust.

- *Dependability, loyalty, ability, attitude, willingness and harmony are the six necessary ingredients to really get cooking.*

- *Meet weekly at a definite time and place to discuss plans and actions.*

- *Be sure that your motive is strong enough to get what you want accomplished.*

2. Remember: these are people you don't want to just get along with but minds you want to unite with in order to help one another solve particular agendas and progress personally and professionally. **Not only will your skills as a transitional thinker develop, but you will experience that joy so rarely felt in school—a cooperative, non-competitive experience of thinking as one person.**

Mentoring

If you try even half of the suggestions in this handbook, you're going to increase your ability to respond to new ideas and new customers a hundredfold. Nevertheless, it's a good idea to have a resource, someone you look up to who has been through it all before. This is the value of a mentor. What do you look for in such a person? Four things:

- **experience;** the experienced are always the best teachers;

- **results;** someone with high integrity, recognized for their achievements;

- **a degree of understanding;** you've got to speak the same language, share the same values;

- **a willingness to listen;** someone older who has already made their mark and feels no competition.

Owner's Manual

1. In NEER-like fashion, target the mentor of your choice.

2. Using the Seven Circles principle, contact that person and ask for a few minutes of their time. Briefly enumerate their accomplishments and why their knowledge and experience seem valuable to you. Then ask if he or she would be willing to share that knowledge with you.

3. Once you have been chosen as a student, you must perfect the art of being mentored. Let respectfulness lead the way. Let honesty, openness and gratitude be the principles by which you conduct yourself. Although our culture does not honor the mentor-student relationship as fully as other cultures through-out the world, recognize this relationship as a most profound exchange.

Keep Your Antennae Up

The real source of all problem-solving, creative prospecting, developing referrals, building a team, NER and NEER marketing, influence leveraging, Master Minding and every other principle discussed in this report is **not found in talking. It's found in listening.**

We've focused on how to add value by going above and beyond the job description and the call of duty, but what this handbook really amounts to is a revolution in the way you perceive the needs of the customer. Being there for the **customer's total business and personal needs** involves learning how to listen in a brand new way. It means a commitment not to be satisfied until the customer is satisfied. And with listening comes greater responsibility. The Japanese have a word for it: *haragei*. It means listening with an open heart, a clear mind and your total body.

Owner's Manual

1. *Keep your antennae up.* Connecting ideas with customers, prospects and suppliers is the one never-ending activity that is the ultimate determination for success. It's the culmination of the previous thirty-nine ideas and the one we'd most like you to remember.

Glossary of Acronyms

We at Planned Marketing have been called masters of the acronym. It isn't just that we have weak memories and can't remember our own terms any other way; we can't get over the power of the subconscious to exert influence over our conscious mind. So the initials strike more than one chord at a time. We ask our readers to beware: we wish to turn the phrase until it catches in your imagination and vibrates violently with a vivid vision.

A-S-K: short for **A**sk and it shall be given; **S**eek and ye shall find; **K**nock and the door shall be opened. From better marriages and family relations to savings on purchases, from a raise in salary to the power of a persuader with a purpose, this little three letter word is your greatest guarantee for success. In terms of conversation dynamics, don't forget that the one asking the questions is the one who controls the direction and outcome of the conversation. At one of our recent Boot Kamps, we were asked why we always answered a question with a question. "We don't know," we said, "why shouldn't we?"

BESA: short for **B**ack **E**nd **S**ales **A**nnuity. This is not just just for sales and marketing folks. It's an attitude, a way to keep customers more fully satisfied by thinking about *all* the goods and services you and your company might provide beyond what the buyers themselves came to purchase.

B-L-T: short for **B**elievability, **L**ikability and **T**rust. From soup to nuts, whatever you're selling has got to come in this package because people buy you and your contagious enthusiasm, not the product or service you represent. In a phrase, Likes Like Likes. While we're on the subject, don't forget the importance of giving the prospect the **Big A's** when doing business: **A**ttention, **A**cceptance, **A**pproval, **A**dmiration, **A**ppreciation and **A**greeability.

BOTSOM: short for **B**ase **O**f **T**hought, **S**tate **O**f **M**ind. You can't change the latter without changing the former. This is a particularly valuable acronym to remember as a persuader. Appeal to the thinking that structures the outlook if you seek to liberate the outlook.

CBS: short for **C**ompelling **B**enefit **S**tatement. Present what your company offers in terms of the key benefits that will compel the prospect to want to know more. It is from such an opener that you can move to PDQ/DMB: **P**robe, **D**iscover and **Q**uestion in order to ascertain the prospect's **D**ominant **B**uying **M**otive. When your **FAB**'s (the **F**eatures of your product, the **A**dvantages of using your product, the **B**enefits for the buyer) correspond with their **DBM**'s, the sale is not far behind.

FEAR: short for **F**alse **E**vidence **A**ppearing **R**eal. Quite often objections to purchasing your products and services are actually nothing more than opportunities for you to remove FEAR. That's why we encourage you to listen with your whole heart and mind.

ICP: short for your **I**deal **C**ustomer **P**rofile. Create a specific picture for the kind of customer you seek. Get demographic! Once you know what your ideal client looks like, you will be able to identify those traits in every prospect you meet. Birds of a feather flock together.

KIS/MIF: short for **K**eep **I**t **S**imple, **M**ake **I**t **F**un. It sounds a lot like Kismet and it's one of our favorite reminders. We think it's the perfect balance for your **MO**—not your **M**odus **O**perandi, but your **M**agnificent **O**bsession, which we also like to call **GAP** or **G**oal **A**ction **P**lan.

NER: short for **N**aturally **E**xisting **R**elationships. This is the essence of our ESP approach. Before you market, advertise and promote your business with big bucks and fancy promotions, first give a call to those people who you already relate to on a regular basis. You believe in what you do and what your company produces, so who are you going to call to help you bring in the business but the people who believe in you?

NEER: short for **N**aturally **E**xisting **E**conomic **R**elationships. This is NER with even more focus. No one wants to see you succeed like the people your company keeps in business by paying money to a regular basis.

PART-NEER: short for **P**rofessional **A**dvisory **R**esearch **T**eam **N**etworking **E**xisting **E**conomic **R**elationships. This is your informal Board of Directors, a group of peers who do not compete with what you do but who help you spread the word.

T.E.A.M.: short for **T**ogether **E**veryone **A**ccomplishes **M**ore. And that's the whole story of ESP. Enough said.